j567.9   Zoehfeld, Kathleen
Z   Weidner.

           Where did dinosaurs
           come from?

$16.99

DATE			

WHERE DID
DINOSAURS
COME FROM?

by Kathleen Weidner Zoehfeld • illustrated by Lucia Washburn

Collins
An Imprint of HarperCollinsPublishers

Special thanks to Dr. Robert T. Bakker
for his unflagging expert attention to this project from start to finish.

And to Dr. Randall Irmis,
whose suggestions helped improve many portions of the text.

The Let's-Read-and-Find-Out Science book series was originated by Dr. Franklyn M. Branley, Astronomer Emeritus and former Chairman of the American Museum–Hayden Planetarium, and was formerly co-edited by him and Dr. Roma Gans, Professor Emeritus of Childhood Education, Teachers College, Columbia University. Text and illustrations for each of the books in the series are checked for accuracy by an expert in the relevant field. For more information about Let's-Read-and-Find-Out Science books, write to HarperCollins Children's Books, 10 East 53rd Street, New York, NY 10022, or visit our website at www.letsreadandfindout.com.

Library of Congress Cataloging-in-Publication Data
Zoehfeld, Kathleen Weidner.
    Where did dinosaurs come from? / by Kathleen Weidner Zoehfeld ; illustrated by Lucia Washburn.—1st ed.
        p.   cm.—(Let's-read-and-find-out science)
    ISBN 978-0-06-029022-1 (trade bdg.) — ISBN 978-0-06-445216-8 (pbk.)
    1. Dinosaurs—Juvenile fiction. 2. Paleontology—Juvenile literature. I. Washburn, Lucia, ill. II. Title. III. Series.
QE861.5.Z65 2011   2009020543
567.9—dc22

Typography by John Sazaklis   11 12 13 14 15   SCP   10 9 8 7 6 5 4 3 2 1   ❖   First Edition

In memory of Frank Branley and Roma Gans
—K.W.Z.

For David
—L.W.

Tyrannosaurus rex

Apatosaurus

8

DINOSAURS! They are the biggest,
scariest creatures that ever walked the Earth.

Apatosaurus. Stegosaurus. Tyrannosaurus rex.
Why did they grow so big? Why are none of them
alive today? There are many dinosaur mysteries.

But here is the biggest mystery of all:
Where did dinosaurs come from?

Stegosaurus

9

4.6 billion years ago
Earth formed

To find out, you have to look way back in time.
Millions of years before the first birds lived
on Earth. Millions and millions of years before
the first dogs or people.

3.5 billion years ago
First single-celled life-forms

540 million years ago
First animals with eyes and brains

PRECAMBRIAN

330 million years ago
First animals to lay eggs on land

450 million years ago
First animals with backbones

65 million years ago
Mammals take over the Earth

370 million years ago
First four-legged animals

PALEOZOIC ERA

TRIASSIC
PERIOD

JURASSIC
PERIOD

CRETACEOUS
PERIOD

MESOZOIC ERA
THE TIME OF DINOSAURS

CENOZOIC
ERA

245 million years ago
Archosaurs begin to take over

208 million years ago
Dinosaurs take over the Earth

144 million years ago

Present day

50 thousand years ago
First modern humans

Fossils help us look back in time.

Fossils are parts of living things that have been preserved in rock. And they give us clues about the long history of life on Earth.

The oldest fossils are stromatolites. They were formed by colonies of tiny, single-celled life-forms. These slimy, blue-green bacteria lived . . .

. . . 3.5 BILLION years ago!

Ever since then, new life-forms have been evolving, while others have been going extinct.

Stromatolites

All the earliest fossils come from creatures that lived in the sea. But it took more than 3 billion years for the first fish to evolve. They were the first animals with backbones.

The first backboned animals to come out of the water and breathe air evolved around 370 million years ago. These animals had four legs. Like many of today's amphibians, they could walk on land, but they had to go back to the water to lay their eggs. For millions of years, strange amphibians ruled the swamps, lakes, and ponds.

What lived their whole lives on land?
Insects and spiders and scorpions!
But no backboned animals could.

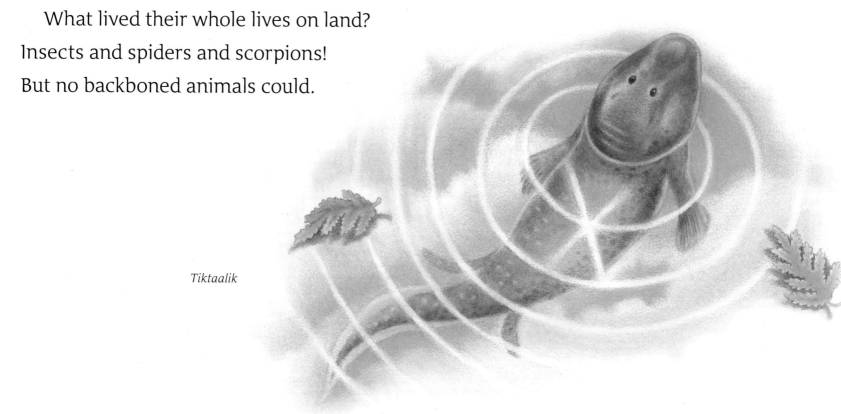

Tiktaalik

Icthyostega

Paleothyris

Then, around 330 million years ago, a new type of animal appeared. Like today's reptiles, these animals could lay tough-shelled eggs on land. That meant they could live on land all the time.

We know that all dinosaurs had backbones, breathed air, and laid their eggs on land. So, an ancient land-loving egg layer must have been the ancestor of the dinosaurs. But it wasn't just any old egg layer!

Hylonomus

Eighty million years passed, and many new egg layers evolved. Two hundred fifty million years ago, four-legged egg layers of all shapes and sizes filled the Earth—weird, two-tusked plant eaters and meat eaters with big, sharp teeth. Look at those saber-toothed gorgons! They must be dinosaur ancestors, right?

Procynosuchus
(a cynodont)

Dicynodon
(a dicynodont)

No! They are relatives of ours—ancestors of the furry mammals.

The two-tusked dicynodonts ate the bushes.

Gorgons and cynodonts ate the dicynodonts. All of them were mammal relatives.

Mammal relatives ruled!

Gorgonops
(a gorgon)

Archosaurus

These early mammal relatives were big and tough. But they could not have been dinosaur ancestors. Fossils tell us why. Here is what a gorgon skull looked like. Notice behind each eye. There is one hole. Cynodont and dicynodont skulls also have one hole behind each eye.

We know that all dinosaurs had TWO holes in their skulls behind each eye. And they had special holes in front of each eye, and in their lower jaws. To trace the origin of dinosaurs, we need to find an ancient ancestor that had those extra holes.

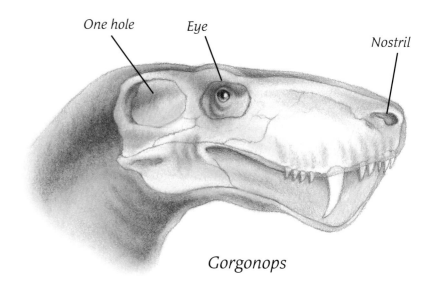

One hole   Eye   Nostril

Gorgonops

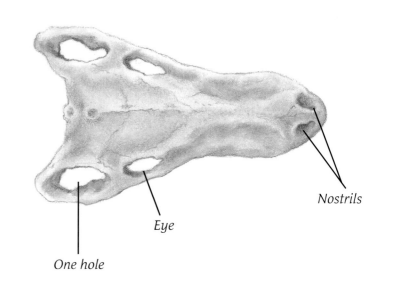

Nostrils

Eye

One hole

A smaller animal called *Archosaurus* lived at the same time as the gorgons. Look at *Archosaurus*'s head. Count the holes in its skull. Nostrils, eye sockets, a little notch for the ear, and . . . there are the extra holes! *Archosaurus* must have been one of the most ancient relatives of dinosaurs.

Aside from the extra holes, it wasn't much like a dinosaur at all. It had four short, sprawling legs and a droopy snout. In spite of its sharp, bladelike teeth, little *Archosaurus* must have been stalked by bigger, fiercer animals day and night.

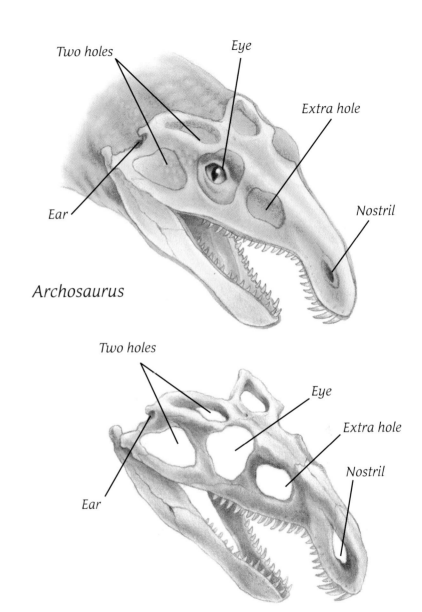

Two holes

Eye

Extra hole

Ear

Nostril

Archosaurus

Two holes

Eye

Extra hole

Nostril

Ear

The word "archo-saur" is Greek for "ruling reptile." But *Archosaurus* probably spent more time hiding in burrows than "ruling" over anything. Nevertheless, it wasn't long before *Archosaurus*'s descendants—a group of animals called archosaurs—really did take over.

By the start of the Triassic Period, 245 million years ago, the world had changed dramatically. Gorgons were gone. Many other types of animals had gone extinct too. Within 10 million years, archosaurs were everywhere.

Poposaurus

Erythrosuchus

Chanaresuchus

By the middle of the Triassic, many different types had evolved. Big or small, they all had those special holes in the skull.

The awesome archosaur *Erythrosuchus* had a head nearly as long as a bathtub. Even though it was one of the biggest, fiercest animals around, it was not quite a dinosaur. Unlike dinosaurs, archosaurs such as *Erythrosuchus* had four short, stumpy legs. And they had strong, straight necks.

Kannemeyeria

Cynognathus

We know that, besides the extra holes in the skull, dinosaurs had hind legs that were longer and more powerful than their front legs. They stood on their toes, with their legs straight underneath their bodies. They had special hingelike joints in their ankles. And they had curving, S-shaped necks.

The first animals to have all or most of these dinosaur-like features were small. They could walk upright on two legs. And all of them were meat eaters.

Eoraptor

One of the earliest dinosaurs appeared about 228 million years ago. We call it *Eoraptor,* or "dawn hunter." Including its long tail and slender neck, it was only about three feet (about one meter) long.

Like the dinosaurs that came after it, *Eoraptor* had those special holes in the skull. It had ankles that moved like hinges to give it extra speed and spring in its step. And it had an S-shaped neck.

Eoraptor had short arms, two long legs, and feet with three main toes. All early meat-eating dinosaurs had these important features, too.

The first dinosaurs were probably the speediest animals around. But life was not easy for them.

By then, the fierce cynodonts had nearly died out. But dangerous new archosaurs had evolved. Some could swallow an *Eoraptor* in one gulp.

Ornithosuchus

Coelophysis

Postosuchus

Giant meat eaters like *Postosuchus* were relatives of today's alligators and crocodiles. These new crocodile-like archosaurs had an upright stance, and they could run almost as fast as dinosaurs.

The earliest dinosaurs eked out a living in a world dominated by big crocodile relatives.

Scaphonyx

Exaeretodon

Stahleckeria

Eoraptor

Desmatosuchus

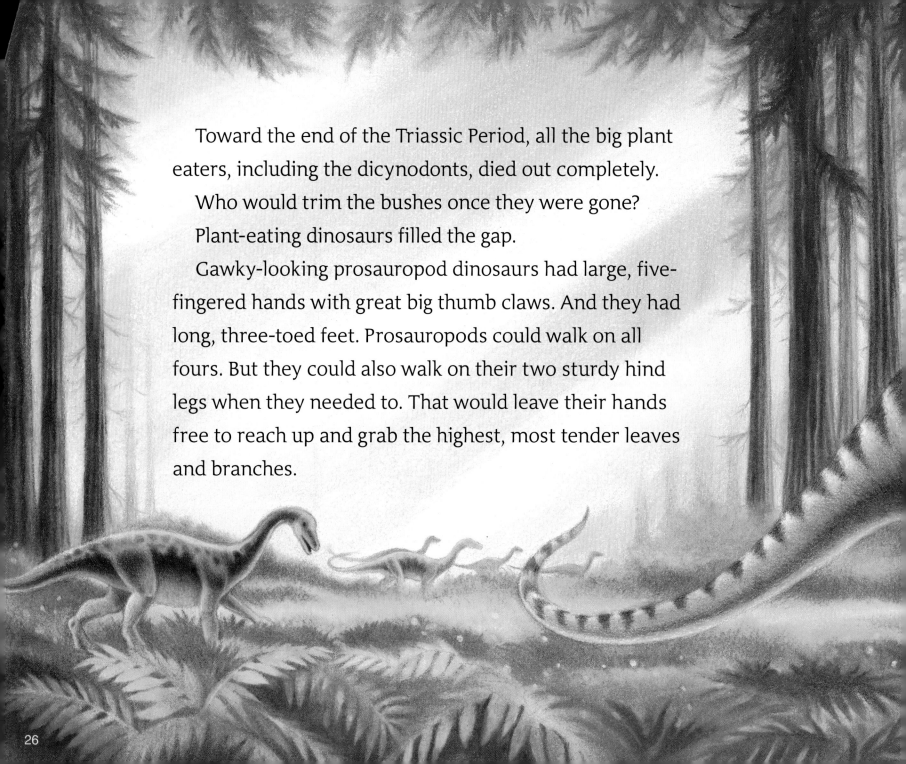

Toward the end of the Triassic Period, all the big plant eaters, including the dicynodonts, died out completely.

Who would trim the bushes once they were gone? Plant-eating dinosaurs filled the gap.

Gawky-looking prosauropod dinosaurs had large, five-fingered hands with great big thumb claws. And they had long, three-toed feet. Prosauropods could walk on all fours. But they could also walk on their two sturdy hind legs when they needed to. That would leave their hands free to reach up and grab the highest, most tender leaves and branches.

Like the earliest meat eaters, most of the earliest prosauropods were small.

The first plant-eating dinosaurs evolved from early meat eaters. But while meat-eating dinosaurs were still rare, plant-eating dinosaurs began to flourish. Within a few million years, prosauropods of all sizes were chomping on the trees and bushes in nearly every corner of the Earth.

Unaysaurus

Plateosaurus

Dilophosaurus

By the start of the Jurassic Period, once again the world had changed. No one has figured out exactly why yet, but—lucky for the dinosaurs—most of the terrible crocodile relatives died out.

Once those big, meat-eating archosaurs went extinct, the speediest meat-eating archosaurs—the dinosaurs— finally began to thrive.

New types of plant-eating dinosaurs began to flourish, too.

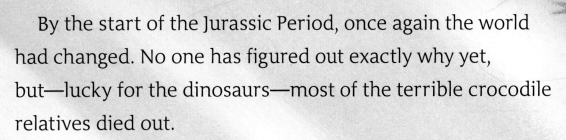

Podokesaurus

Scutellosaurus

By the middle of the Jurassic, around 180 million years ago, most of the early types of dinosaurs had gone extinct. During the Jurassic, all over the Earth, new dinosaurs were evolving.

Brachiosaurus

Where herds of prosauropods once roamed, now there were herds of huge sauropods. Sauropods are the biggest land animals that have ever lived.

These giants walked on four legs, but it's easy to see they came from two-legged ancestors. The front legs of sauropods are more slender than their hind legs. Some sauropods could even rear up on their hefty hind legs to reach the highest trees.

Apatosaurus

Some of the biggest meat eaters the Earth has ever seen evolved in the Jurassic. Megalosaurs and allosaurs were very similar to the earliest meat-eating dinosaurs. They had short arms, long legs, and feet with three main toes. But they were much, MUCH bigger.

By that time, many types of dinosaurs had developed interesting new features. Some plant eaters, like *Stegosaurus*, grew spikes and tall plates to help keep those enormous meat eaters away.

Torvosaurus

Camptosaurus

Ornitholestes

Smaller meat-eating dinosaurs developed
a useful body covering called . . . feathers!
Birds, the most modern archosaurs of all,
evolved from these dinosaurs.

Foxraptor

Stegosaurus

Allosaurus

Pediomys

Bambiraptor

If the meat-eating dinosaurs of the Jurassic were big, those of the Cretaceous Period were humongous! *Tyrannosaurus rex* lived near the end of the Cretaceous—67 million years ago.

Plant-eating dinosaurs had to evolve powerful defenses against these giants. *Triceratops* had long, sharp horns, and the armored *Ankylosaurus* could swing the big club at the end of its tail.

Ankylosaurus

Edmontosaurus

Other animals hid out in burrows or clung to the safety of the trees and bushes. From the start of the Jurassic until the end of the Cretaceous—when all the big dinosaurs went extinct—our ancestors lived in hiding. Hardly any mammal grew larger than a squirrel.

This was the Time of Dinosaurs!

Tyrannosaurus rex

Triceratops

Didelphodon

PALEOZOIC		MESOZOIC—The Time of Dinosaurs			CENOZOIC

/ 360 million years ago
CARBONIFEROUS

/ 295 million years ago
PERMIAN

/ 245 million years ago
TRIASSIC

/ 208 million years ago
JURASSIC

/ 144 million years ago
CRETACEOUS

/ 65 million years ago
TERTIARY

PRESENT DAY

Tetrapods
(animals with four limbs)

Amniotes
(animals that lay tough-shelled,
air-breathing eggs)

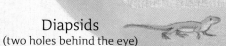

Synapsids (one hole behind the eye)

Diapsids
(two holes behind the eye)

Reptiles

Archosaurs

Crocodilians

Pterosaurs

Dinosaurs

Ornithischian
dinosaurs

Saurischian
dinosaurs

Sauropods

Theropods (meat-eating dinosaurs)

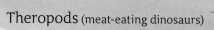

Birds

36

Glossary

Animals are listed as they appear in illustrations, from left to right. The sizes listed represent the biggest adult fossils that have been found. A metric ton is slightly larger than a U.S. ton. All tons are U.S. tons.

Pages 12–13

Tiktaalik (tick-TAH-lick): This 375-million-year-old fish had leglike fins. It could grow up to 9 feet (3 meters) long.

Icthyostega (ick-thee-oh-STEG-ah): One of the first animals with four real legs; its fingers and toes did not have claws. It had short legs and was a slow waddler. It was about 5 feet (1.5 meters) long.

Pages 14–15

Paleothyris (pale-ee-oh-THY-riss): An insect eater with a strong backbone and legs for walking on land, and claws on its fingers and toes. It was about 12 inches (30 centimeters) long.

Hylonomus (hi-LON-uh-muss): Like *Paleothyris*, this insect eater's skull and neck and other bones resembled a lizard's. Like a lizard, it probably laid eggs on land. It grew to about 9 inches (20 centimeters) long.

Pages 16–17

Procynosuchus (pro-sine-uh-SOOK-us): A cynodont—a meat-eating early mammal relative that, much like today's mammals, may have been covered by fur. It grew to about 2.5 feet (76 centimeters) long and weighed 20 pounds (9 kilograms).

Dicynodon (die-SINE-uh-don): A dicynodont—a two-tusked, plant-eating mammal relative. It was 5 feet (1.5 meters) long and weighed 250 pounds (113 kilograms).

Gorgonops (GORE-gun-ops): A tiger-sized, meat-eating early mammal relative. It was 9 feet (3 meters) long and 300 pounds (136 kilograms).

Archosaurus (ark-oh-SORE-us): The first archosaur; known from only a few scraps of bone. Unlike the early mammal relatives, most archosaurs had stronger back legs than front legs. It probably grew to about 6 feet (2 meters) long and weighed about 50 pounds (23 kilograms).

Pages 20–21

Poposaurus (PO-po-sore-us): A large meat-eating archosaur. Like many of the large archosaurs, it could rear up on its two strong hind legs. It was 16 feet (5 meters) long and weighed as much as 1,000 pounds (.5 ton).

Erythrosuchus (eh-reeth-roe-SOOK-us): A meat-eating archosaur with saw-edged teeth; it could grow as long as 13 feet (4 meters) and weighed up to 1,000 pounds (.5 ton).

Chanaresuchus (chan-ah-re-SOOK-us): A small, long-legged, droopy-snouted archosaur, about 5 feet (1.5 meters) long and 35 pounds (16 kilograms).

Kannemeyeria (can-eh-my-ERR-ee-ah): An ox-sized dicynodont, about 8 feet (2.5 meters) long and 1,000 pounds (.5 ton).

Cynognathus (sine-oh-NAY-thus): A leopard-sized, meat-eating cynodont, about 7 feet (2 meters) long and 150 pounds (68 kilograms).

Pages 24–25

Ornithosuchus (or-nith-uh-SOOK-us): A meat-eating archosaur that was 12 feet (4 meters) long and weighed 800 pounds (363 kilograms).

Coelophysis (see-low-FY-sis): An early meat-eating dinosaur that could walk on its two hind legs. It was about 10 feet (3 meters) long and 110 pounds (50 kilograms).

Postosuchus (POST-uh-sook-us): A meat-eating archosaur that was the top predator of its day; it could grow up to 20 feet (6 meters) long and weighed 1,500 pounds (.75 ton).

Scaphonyx (scaf-ON-icks): A tweezer-beaked plant eater and a close archosaur relative. It was about 7 feet (2 meters) long and 200 pounds (90 kilograms).

Exaeretodon (ex-ah-REE-toe-don): A plant-eating cynodont. It was about 7 feet (2 meters) long and 200 pounds (90 kilograms).

Eoraptor (EE-oh-rap-tor): A light, speedy meat-eating dinosaur. It was about 3 feet (1 meter) long and weighed about 50 pounds (23 kilograms).

Stahleckeria (stal-ek-ERR-ee-ah): A rhino-sized dicynodont, about 12 feet (4 meters) long and weighing up to a ton.

Desmatosuchus (des-mat-uh-SOOK-us): A large, spiky plant-eating archosaur covered with armor plate. It was about 12 feet (4 meters) long and weighed 1,500 pounds (.75 ton).

Pages 26–27

Plateosaurus (PLAT-ee-oh-sore-us): One of the biggest prosauropods. It was about 27 feet (8 meters) long and weighed up to 2 tons.

Unaysaurus (yoo-nay-SORE-us): A small plant-eating prosauropod. It was about 8 feet (2.5 meters) long and weighed about 155 pounds (70 kilograms).

Pages 28–29

Dilophosaurus (die-LOF-uh-sore-us): One of the first big meat-eating dinosaurs. It was 20 feet (6 meters) long and weighed more than 800 pounds (363 kilograms).

Scutellosaurus (SCUTE-el-uh-sore-us): A small plant-eating dinosaur that was one of the first to develop armor. It was 4.5 feet (1.5 meters) long and weighed 44 pounds (20 kilograms).

Podokesaurus (poe-DOKE-ee-sore-us): A small meat-eating dinosaur that may have hunted in packs. It was about 3.5 feet (1 meter) long and weighed 25 pounds (12 kilograms).

Pages 30–31

Brachiosaurus (BRAK-ee-oh-sore-us): A plant-eating sauropod. It was 82 feet (25 meters) long and weighed 50 to 80 tons.

Apatosaurus (ah-PAT-uh-sore-us): A plant-eating sauropod. It was 80 feet (24 meters) long and weighed 30 tons.

Pages 32–33

Torvosaurus (TOR-voe-soar-us): A hefty, meat-eating megalosaurid dinosaur. It was 30 feet (9 meters) long and weighed 4 tons.

Ornitholestes (or-nith-uh-LESS-tees): A feathered meat-eating dinosaur; it was 4 feet (1 meter) long and weighed 50 pounds (23 kilograms).

Camptosaurus (CAMP-toe-sore-us): A two-legged plant-eating dinosaur that lived in herds for safety. It was 16–20 feet (5–6 meters) long and weighed up to half a ton.

Stegosaurus (steg-uh-SORE-us): A plant-eating dinosaur. It was 24 feet (7 meters) long and weighed 5 tons.

Allosaurus (AL-uh-sore-us): A meat-eating allosaurid dinosaur. It was 30–40 feet (9–12 meters) long and weighed 2 tons.

Foxraptor (FOX-rap-tor): While cynodonts and other early mammal relatives had become extinct, mammals that looked more like the mammals we know today had evolved. Most, like this one, were very small—about the size of a mouse. It was about 5 inches (13 centimeters) long and weighed about 0.6 ounces (17 grams).

Pages 34–35

Bambiraptor (BAM-bee-rap-tor): A small, feathered, meat-eating dinosaur. It was 3 feet (1 meter) long and weighed 25 pounds (12 kilograms).

Pediomys (peed-ee-OH-mees): A mouse-sized mammal that lived in trees and bushes. It was about 5 inches (13 centimeters) long and weighed about 0.6 ounces (17 grams).

Ankylosaurus (an-KYE-low-sore-us): An armored plant-eating dinosaur. It was about 20–30 feet (6–9 meters) long and weighed 3–4 tons.

Edmontosaurus (ed-MON-tuh-sore-us): A duck-billed plant-eating dinosaur that lived in herds. It was about 43 feet (13 meters) long and weighed 4 tons.

Triceratops (try-SER-ah-tops): A horned plant-eating dinosaur. It was 26–30 feet (8–9 meters) long and weighed 6–12 tons.

Tyrannosaurus rex (tuh-RAN-uh-sore-us REX): One of the largest meat-eating dinosaurs ever. It was 43 feet (13 meters) long and weighed 6–7 tons.

Didelphodon (die-DELF-uh-don): One of the fiercest mammals of its time; the largest were about the size of a Tasmanian devil. It was 25 inches (64 centimeters) long and weighed 18 pounds (8 kilograms).